Frank M. Johnson, Jr.
Courageous Judge

Frank Sikora
Michelle Batcheler

Seacoast Publishing
Birmingham, Alabama

Frank M. Johnson, Jr.: Courageous Judge

Published by Seacoast Publishing, Inc.
1149 Mountain Oaks Drive
Birmingham, Alabama 35226

Copyright © 2009 Frank Sikora and Michelle Batcheler

All rights reserved.
Reviewers and writers of magazine and newspaper articles are free to quote passages of this book as needed for their work. Otherwise, no part of this book may be reproduced or transmitted in any form or by any means, electronic or mechanical, including photocopying, recording or by any information storage and retrieval system, without the written permission of the publisher.

Library of Congress Control Number: 2008937555

Cover art by Thomas B. Moore

ISBN 1-59421-045-4

Photographs courtesy of the Johnson family.

To obtain copies of this book, please write or call:
Seacoast Publishing, Inc.
Post Office Box 26492
Birmingham, Alabama 35260
(205) 979-2909

Frank Sikora and Michelle Batcheler

Dedication

To Mom and Dad for their unconditional love, and my fiance Daniel.

—Michelle Batcheler

To Josephine and John Sikora.

—Frank Sikora

Frank M. Johnson, Jr.: Courageous Judge

About The Series

Alabama Roots is a book series designed to provide reading pleasure for young people, to allow readers to better know the men and women who shaped the State of Alabama, and to fill a much-needed void of quality regional non-fiction for students in middle grades.

For years, teachers and librarians have searched for quality biographies about famous people from Alabama. This series is a response to that search. The series will cover a span of time from pre-statehood through the modern day.

The goal of *Alabama Roots* is to provide biographies that are historically accurate and as interesting as the characters whose lives they explore.

The *Alabama Roots* mark assures readers and educators of consistent quality in research, composition, and presentation.

It is a joint publishing project of Seacoast Publishing, Inc., and Will Publishing, Inc., both located in Birmingham, Alabama.

Frank Sikora and Michelle Batcheler

Writing This Book

While a reporter for *The Birmingham News*, Frank Sikora spent more time with Frank Johnson and interviewed him as much if not more than any other reporter in America. For this book, Frank and Michelle Batcheler relied on Sikora's years of interviews with Judge Johnson, court records, newspaper accounts, and the other books written about the judge.

While those writings have been aimed at an adult audience, there has been little written about Johnson for younger readers. That is the goal of this book. It is hoped it will bring a better understanding of the Civil Rights Movement in the South, much of it centered in Alabama, and the vital role Judge Johnson played in it.

The authors visited Montgomery and Johnson's home town of Haleyville as well as the Selma-to-Montgomery Historic Trail to capture the spirit of Judge Johnson's life and the impact he had on the lives of so many.

Books that were used as resources include:

Tinsley E. Yarbrough, *Judge Frank Johnson and Human Rights in Alabama*, (University of Alabama Press).

Robert F. Kennedy, Jr., *Judge Frank Johnson*, (Putnam).

Frank Sikora, *The Judge, The Life & Opinions of Alabama's Frank M. Johnson, Jr.*, (Black Belt Press)

Jack Bass, *Taming The Storm, The Life And Times of Judge Frank M. Johnson, Jr. And The South's Fight Over Civil Rights,* (Doubleday)

Judge Frank Johnson: Antics and Anecdotes, (private publication by the law clerks)

Foreword

It is March 11, 1965, a muggy Thursday in Montgomery, the capital of Alabama. The morning is cloudy; rain is in the forecast.

At the United States Courthouse, a tan building with magnolia trees in the front lawn, a crowd has gathered for a hearing.

A judge is to decide if hundreds of people can march from Selma to Montgomery along U.S. 80, a distance of fifty miles.

The nation—in fact much of the world—is watching to see what will happen in Alabama.

In Selma the Sunday before, March 7, about 600 black people and a few white people tried such a journey. As they crossed a bridge, Alabama State Troopers charged into them. Behind the troopers galloped mounted sheriff's deputies.

That night millions of Americans saw television scenes of lawmen hitting marchers who ran screaming through clouds of tear gas.

Frank M. Johnson, Jr.: Courageous Judge

Now the judge enters the courtroom.

"All rise!" barks the bailiff.

U.S. District Judge Frank M. Johnson Jr., 46, is a tall, craggy-faced man with thick, brown hair and narrow piercing eyes. He sits down behind the broad oak bench.

"All right gentlemen, we are ready to proceed," he says, peering over his half-rim glasses. His voice is low but firm, and has a hillbilly twang to it. "Call your first witness."

Attorney Fred Gray stands. "We call Dr. Martin Luther King, Jr."

King testifies that a march will dramatize the fact that blacks cannot vote in Selma nor much of the rural South.

An attorney for the State of Alabama argues that King broke the law when he led marches in Selma. A Selma judge had banned public meetings.

"That's right," King agrees. "Well, we went on—"

"Wait a minute," attorney McLean Pitts says. "And you knew that and you marched and carried signs—"

"That's right, I—"

"I am going to ask you…and you walked in the middle of the streets, didn't you?" Pitts accuses.

"At first we walked on the sidewalks," King explains.

"Now listen," the attorney scolds, "you walked all the way from the depot to Broad Street in the middle of the street, didn't you?"

"Well, I don't know what happened behind," King says, "but I am saying that in front of the line—"

Pitts cuts him off again. "I am going to ask you one more time, you, yourself, marched in the middle of Water Street—"

"Wait a minute," the judge says. He fixes a frosty gaze on Pitts. "All witnesses in this court, regardless of who they are, are to be questioned with common courtesy."

"I am trying, your honor," Pitts says meekly. "But—"

"Make a little better effort!" Johnson snaps.

The crisp tone brings a murmur from the spectators. Now the judge shifts his gaze to them. In a stern voice he warns, "We will keep order in this court or you will be excluded."

There isn't a sound. Not even a bench creaks.

"All right," the judge says, speaking to Pitts. "Let's get along."

* * *

The Selma-to-Montgomery March hearing was just one

Frank M. Johnson, Jr.: Courageous Judge

of a number of civil rights cases that Judge Frank Johnson heard during the 1950s and '60s.

To some it seemed fate had placed Johnson in Montgomery at the moment in American history when the Civil Rights Movement began.

Frank Johnson was chosen to be a federal judge by President Dwight Eisenhower and was sworn in on Nov. 7, 1955.

In less than a month, an African American woman named Rosa Parks was arrested on a Montgomery bus when she refused the bus driver's order to give her seat to a white person.

It would lead to a massive boycott of Montgomery buses by blacks; overnight 30,000 would stop riding. In those days in Alabama and other Southern states, the law was based on segregation—keeping black and white people separated.

"Separate but equal." was the law as well as social custom. Blacks could not eat in most restaurants, nor vote; could not use restrooms at most service stations, not attend white schools; had to sit in the balcony at movie theaters, and had to ride in the back of the bus.

And if they were called as witnesses in court cases, attorneys often treated them with scorn.

This was one of the practices that would change when Frank Johnson became a federal judge. He would change others...

Chapter 1

FRANK MINIS JOHNSON JR., was born Oct. 30, 1918, in the rural hamlet of Delmar, Alabama, in Winston County.

Set in the northwest corner of the state, Winston County was rugged land with rocky hills, hardwood hollows, whispering streams with waterfalls, and only an occasional meadow. There were few farms, most of which were small.

His parents, Frank M. Johnson Sr., and Alabama Long Johnson, were school teachers.

Frank was the first of seven children. While he was still a toddler, the family moved to nearby Haleyville, the largest town in the county. His father became the postmaster there.

As Frank started school, he began to develop a sense of responsibility.

"I had to learn it," he said years later. "When you have that many brothers and sisters you have to help your mother. And I did. I had to help take care of the

Frank M. Johnson, Jr.: Courageous Judge

Toddler Frank Johnson with his mother.

younger ones."

One day his mother became concerned when he did not arrive home from school at the usual time.

She walked down the road looking for him. A neighbor told her that some people were gathering crops in a nearby field. Mrs. Johnson hurried to the place. Sure enough, there was young Frank picking peas "on the halves." It meant he could keep half of what he picked.

His mother smiled when she saw him, saying to the neighbor: "He may never amount to much, but he'll work hard at it."

The family had peas for supper that evening, and Frank made some money selling what his mother did not cook. It meant he would have a dime to go to the

Princess Theater on Saturday to see a cowboy movie.

In the summers, Frank would spend several weeks with his grandparents. One summer he learned carpentry, helping his grandfather build a barn. It was a craft that he would use though his life.

"Keep those edges straight," his grandfather would tell him. "Make sure it's lined up."

Frank learned quickly and took pride in his work. "I always thought I might make a pretty good living being a carpenter," he said in later years.

During those summer visits he would also learn about his heritage. His grandmother, Bessie Johnson, would tell him about the Civil War, when Alabama and other Southern states had split away [seceded] from the United States. The South's move to leave the Union followed the 1860 election of Abraham Lincoln as president. Lincoln opposed slavery, which was vital to the South's cotton economy.

One of Johnson's great-grandfathers had been a soldier for the South. Another fought for the North.

As she talked about those years, his grandmother kneaded dough for biscuits. Often she hummed the "Battle Hymn of the Republic," the anthem of the Union, or the Northern states. Most of Frank's ancestors were loyal to the Union and President Abraham Lincoln.

"One of the issues of the war was slavery," Johnson later recalled. "There were not many slaves in Winston County. The land wasn't much good for farming. So when the Civil War started, the people of Winston County didn't want any part of the war. They wanted to be left alone. So they tried to secede from Alabama."

That is how the county became known as "the Free State of Winston." Many of the men went off to take part in that war, mostly for the North.

After the Civil War the county was known for its self-reliant, hard-working people who did not always agree with the rest of Alabama. While most of the state's white people were Democrats, in Winston County, which was mostly white, the majority was Republican. Frank Johnson later clarified their position:

"We were what I called 'Lincoln Republicans'," he said.

Chapter 2

AS A STUDENT in Haleyville public schools, Frank Johnson did not do as well as his parents had hoped. He was not very good at math or science, but did above-average work in some of the other subjects,

Frank, far right, with brothers and pet dog.

such as civics and history, his favorite. A quiet student who usually sat in the back of the room, Frank seldom raised his hand to answer a teacher's question. But he did well in classroom debates.

By the time he reached the ninth grade, he had grown into a lanky fellow who liked to fish, play football and ride horses. A member of the 4-H Club (an organization for students planning to be farmers when they grew up), he worked hard in the family garden, helping his mother raise corn, tomatoes and beans. He also cared for a horse and cow his father bought.

It was shortly after entering Haleyville High School that an air show was held at a place called Tuggles Pasture, on the outskirts of town. Such shows were popular in rural areas in the 1930s. The shows featured World War I veterans who had learned their flying skills in combat over France. Frank rode the horse to Tuggles Pasture to see the show.

Among those who watched the planes swoop and dive over the field was Ruth Jenkins. A slim, pretty girl with brunette hair, she was a year younger than Frank, but was in some classes with him.

As she watched the airplanes, her attention moved to the young man who had trotted up on the horse.

"Look at him," she said to a friend. "Who does he

think he is?"

"That's Frank Johnson," the friend replied.

"I know who he is," Ruth said. "But why does he have to look so high and mighty just because he has a horse."

Despite her rueful tone, she did find the boy handsome. And Frank Johnson soon took note of her. Not long after that, classmates noticed that Frank was carrying Ruth's books as he walked her home. The two became close friends.

While Frank struggled in the classroom, Ruth became an honor student. Trying to keep up with Ruth turned Frank into a more serious student. He also admired her ability to deal with some of life's tough lessons.

Ruth's father

Portrait of Frank as a young man.

had left the family when she was a little girl. It forced her mother to scrape out a living working at a restaurant. Ruth and her older sisters had to learn to take care of the house and cook.

During the Great Depression of the 1930s, many Americans, who had lost their jobs, roamed the land looking for work or a free meal. Some of them passed through Haleyville.

One day Ruth's mother told Ruth and her sisters: "If anyone comes by and asks for something to eat, give them a bowl of beans and some cornbread. Let them sit on the porch and eat. And if it is a black man, you treat him the same as a white."

She then added: "You're not any better than anyone else. But you're just as good."

Chapter 3

BY 1934 FRANK JOHNSON was a regular on the Haleyville High School Lions football team, playing end. He was good at catching passes, and he hoped one day to earn a college scholarship.

Meantime, his father had been elected probate judge of Winston County. Frank's first interest in the law came on the days he went with his father to the courthouse in Double Springs. There he would spend hours watching trials. He enjoyed listening to the lawyers as they debated cases.

He and Ruth were going steady, attending church and social events together. Then one evening they went for a drive in Mr. Johnson's car. As they talked, Frank failed to see a curve ahead. Suddenly, the car was going off the road. It came to rest in a ditch. Luckily, neither was hurt. But the car was heavily damaged.

Frank's father gave him a stern lecture that night. About a week after the car had been repaired, Frank and two buddies went for a ride. Once again he lost control and it went off the road, taking out a good portion of a rail fence.

His father decided two wrecks was two too many. He sent Frank to a military academy in Gulfport, Mississippi. There, he finished high school.

Coming home, he chose to attend Birmingham-Southern College. While not sure about his career, he knew that he wanted to play football. "I had these long legs and I could run fast," he said. "I liked to chase after those long passes."

But shortly after he enrolled, Birmingham-Southern dropped its football program, and Frank soon left the college. He took classes at Massey Business College in Birmingham. The school produced many of the secretaries and bookkeepers in Alabama.

"It was some of the best training I ever got," he said later. "I learned to type pretty fast."

Soon he landed a job as a bookkeeper with a Birmingham insurance company. With a job and his own apartment, Frank went back to Haleyville and asked Ruth to marry him.

He was 19; she was 18. At first their families did not want them to take such a serious step, but they finally gave in.

On January 16, 1938, Frank and Ruth drove to

Birmingham.

"I wore a blue suit," he recalled, "and Ruth had an outfit that was a lighter blue. We were looking for a preacher who used to live in Winston County. But we couldn't find his church."

Finally they stopped at a church and told the minister they wanted to get married. It was starting to get late in the day. The minister agreed to perform the ceremony, having some of his family members stand in as witnesses. After the vows were exchanged, Frank and Ruth drove the car back to Haleyville. A relative drove them back to Birmingham the next day.

But things soon went bad for the newlyweds. The marriage promptly led to Frank getting fired from his bookkeeping job. His boss told him, "Since you're married now, we're going to let you go. We can't pay you enough to support a family and we're afraid you might be tempted to steal from us."

Nearly broke and without a car, Frank called his family in Winston County for help. He and Ruth packed their belongings and then waited for a ride. With their last 20 cents, they bought two bottles of Royal Crown Cola and a bag of peanuts. "We picked Royal Crown," he explained later, "because it had the biggest bottles."

A relative arrived several hours later and took

Frank M. Johnson, Jr.: Courageous Judge

them to Carbon Hill, about fifty miles northwest of Birmingham. There they stayed with Frank's grandparents.

In a few days, Frank found that his skill as a carpenter paid off. A federal program started by President Franklin Roosevelt put him to work. The idea was to provide jobs for people and help the country get out of the Depression.

The job Frank got was building outhouses—outdoor toilets—for homes across northwest Alabama. He was so good that he was soon was promoted to supervisor, earning $200 a month—good pay during those tough economic times.

"I knew about carpentry because my grandfather had taught me when we built that barn," he said. "I think every boy should help his grandpa build a barn."

Most people at that time did not have indoor plumbing, and many did not have an outhouse. So Frank and his crew went to work building dozens of them across Walker and Fayette counties. He was proud of his work.

In later years, when he and family members drove through that area, he would point to outhouses and declare, "I built that one, and that one over there."

After a year of building outdoor toilets, Frank

made a decision about his future. Arriving at home one evening, he told Ruth, "I think I want to do more in this life than build outhouses."

In the past he had told her that he wanted to be a lawyer. He had said it in a casual way. But now he was more serious. Ruth wasn't sure he would make a good lawyer, but she agreed that it promised a better future than building outhouses.

The next weekend, Frank's parents drove to Carbon Hill to visit. He told them about his plan to study law. Mr. Johnson thought it was a great idea and added that Ruth could get a job while Frank went to classes.

"No, no!" said Frank's mother, who stomped her feet to make her point.

"What's the matter?" asked Frank's father.

"If anyone goes to college it should be Ruth," Mrs. Johnson declared. "She's smart."

"We both want to go," said Frank.

A settlement was reached. The parents said if both wanted to attend college, they would help pay the tuition.

In September 1939, Frank and Ruth entered the University of Alabama. Frank enrolled in the pre-law program, while Ruth decided to take courses leading to a degree in history.

Frank M. Johnson, Jr.: Courageous Judge

They rented an apartment on the outskirts of the campus. Both studied hard and found part-time jobs. Ruth graded papers for a professor, while Frank was hired by the University as a carpenter, repairing furniture, windows and leaky roofs.

As they went about the day-to-day life as students, they knew that all was not well in the world.

On Sept. 1, 1939, Adolph Hitler, the leader of Nazi Germany, sent his army across the Polish border. It was the spark that ignited World War II. Frank and Ruth knew that one day the fighting would affect them and thousands of other young Americans.

That day came on Dec. 7, 1941, a Sunday.

It was a day that Frank and Ruth were having a late lunch. Suddenly, the music on the radio stopped and the announcer read a bulletin.

"Did you hear that?" Ruth asked.

They turned the radio up louder and listened: Japanese aircraft had attacked the U.S. Navy base at Pearl Harbor in the Hawaiian Islands. America was at war.

Like millions of others, Frank and Ruth sat by the radio for hours listening for the latest reports. There was no television in Alabama in the early 1940s. Now, Frank and Ruth were certain their lives would change.

Frank Sikora and Michelle Batcheler

Frank and Ruth Johnson (center) with friends, including fellow law school student George C. Wallace (to Ruth's left)—a man whose friendship would not last.

Four days later, Hitler declared war on America.

At first, the conflict did not have a direct impact on their lives. They continued their college work. But they knew one day Frank would have to go into military service. In 1942 Ruth graduated and was invited by the University faculty to go into a program for an advanced degree. However, money was so short that she decided it would be best if she found a job. She decided to become a teacher in the Tuscaloosa County school system.

One of her students was a girl named Lurleen

Burns. And one of Frank's friends in law school was a feisty young man named George C. Wallace. Wallace would one day marry Lurleen Burns.

In the years ahead, both George and Lurleen would be elected governor of Alabama.

Frank did not take time off in the summers, but continued his studies for the entire year. In the spring of 1943 he was ready to graduate. He knew that as soon as that happened, he would enlist in the Army.

Chapter 4

A FEW WEEKS BEFORE he was to graduate, Ruth said to Frank, "Since you'll be leaving for the Army, I don't want to be left behind. I want to join the Navy WAVES."

The WAVES was the women's branch of the Navy, and thousands of women joined.

Frank agreed with her decision. They had no children and both wanted to do their part in the war. Ruth was assigned to duty in Miami, Florida, and then later to Washington, D.C. A few weeks after she entered the service, Frank joined the Army.

After basic training, he was sent to Fort Benning, Georgia to Officer Candidate School. He became the top soldier in his class. "I enjoyed all the running and the physical training, the climbing and the obstacle courses," he said. "I found it enjoyable."

He graduated from the training class as a second lieutenant, the Army's lowest rank for officers. He was sent to England in early 1944 and assigned to be a platoon leader in the 5th Infantry Division. A platoon is made up of 40 men.

For many months the U.S. and Great Britain had been preparing to invade France, which had been held by Hitler's forces since 1940. On June 6, 1944, American and British troops invaded the Normandy section of France in what became known as D-Day.

Johnson's unit was put on alert to cross the English Channel. In late June, he and his men were ordered to board ships and were on their way to the fighting. They saw combat against German troops in the rolling farmland of France, a region where fields are laced by lines of thickets and small trees, called hedgerows.

One sunny day after weeks of fighting, Johnson's unit was given a brief rest back from the front lines. He saw an Army ration truck and found a jar of orange marmalade, a food like jelly. He sat down in the grass and ate. Then, he stretched out and fell asleep. A short time later he was rudely awakened by five or six honeybees. They were crawling on his face, trying to get to the marmalade.

Fighting in France, Johnson was wounded twice. The first time was near Paris, when a bullet from a

German machine gun hit him. After a week in a field hospital, he went back into combat.

In the winter of 1944-45 American troops fought their way into Germany. Johnson's unit was ordered to attack an enemy stronghold.

"The Germans were firing artillery shells at us," Johnson recalled. "They fired them (on a straight line) right down our throats."

Metal fragments—called shrapnel—from an exploding shell hit Johnson. The impact knocked him on his back. This wound was more serious than the first.

He was sent to an Army hospital in England. By the time he recovered, Germany had surrendered. The war in Europe was over. He carried part of the German shell in his body the rest of his life.

In 1946 Frank Johnson came home to America. He stopped in Washington D.C. where Ruth was still on duty with the Navy. He went to several offices looking for her. In one of them he was met by a Navy officer. Johnson saluted and said, "Sir, I came by to get my wife."

As she came to the office, both of them laughed:

"I outrank you," cried Ruth, who was a commander.

Frank, who was a captain, said, "You do and you

always will."

After she was discharged from the service, they came home to Winston County.

Chapter 5

A SHORT TIME AFTER RETURNING to civilian life, a 27-year-old Johnson went to work with the law firm of James Curtis and Herman Maddox in Jasper, a town in Walker County. Curtis, who was nearly 80, had been a state judge in his younger years.

Frank and Ruth rented an apartment and quickly bought furniture with money that the military gave them. It included a new Stromberg-Carlson radio and record player. They also bought a new car, a Hudson. One night after shopping for groceries, they decided to go to a restaurant for a steak dinner.

As they ate, they heard sirens. Looking out the window they saw a fire truck racing down the street. "I bet that's our apartment," Ruth joked.

"I don't care if it is," Frank replied, grinning. "I'm not leaving until I finish this steak."

As it turned out, it *was* their apartment.

After the steak dinner, they drove home and found the street blocked by police. They learned that the fire started when some boys set off fireworks. One of the sputtering rockets flew through an open window in the apartment below the Johnson's apartment. The fire spread quickly and destroyed all the apartments.

"We didn't have a dime's worth of insurance," he recalled. "We lost everything we had: our clothes; the radio; everything."

Once again the two had to spend some time living with relatives. A few days later they found another apartment. They also decided it was time to get a house, and soon bought a newly-built home.

It looked like Frank and Ruth would settle down in Jasper for the rest of their lives.

While Frank was busy with his law practice, Ruth

Frank as a young lawyer.

went back to teaching history.

One day Frank heard there was a golf tournament in Jasper. He decided to enter and soon found himself in the finals. He played for three straight days.

When he finally returned to his law office, the senior partner, James Curtis, asked to see him.

"Yes, sir," Johnson said, as he entered Mr. Curtis's office.

"Frank," the elderly attorney said in a grave tone. "I think the time has come for you to make a decision."

"What's that, judge?" he asked.

"You need to decide if you're going to spend your time hitting golf balls or practicing law," Curtis said.

Johnson nodded. "Sir, I think I'll practice law."

After that he did not play golf again for nearly ten years.

While Jasper had a population that was mostly white, Frank Johnson soon had his first case involving an African American. A man came to his office one day and told him that the Jasper police had arrested a black man.

"What did he do?" Frank asked.

"Don't know," came the reply. "He's in the jail. He asked if you would come see him."

Frank M. Johnson, Jr.: Courageous Judge

While Frank had never had much contact with black people—few lived in Winston County—he felt that they had not been treated fairly in Alabama. He went to the jail to see the man.

"What did you do?" he asked.

The man replied that he had stood by the railroad tracks holding a pole with a piece of cloth tied to it. Each time a train came by he waved the pole.

It angered Johnson that the police had arrested him.

A friend asked Johnson, "Why was he out there waving a pole?"

"I didn't ask him," Johnson replied. "It makes no difference why he did it. It was not against the law. He didn't do anything."

Frank went to the Jasper city attorney's office and left a written note demanding that the man be freed. If not, he intended to file suit against the city, he said.

After he returned to the office he was told a messenger brought him a note from the city attorney. It said simply, "The man has been released from jail."

That ended Frank Johnson's first civil rights case.

Meanwhile, Ruth was getting involved in a project to help black people in Jasper.

"There was a public library in town," Ruth said, "but many black people felt they were not welcome there."

So she and some other women decided to make a library out of an old block building in Jasper's black neighborhood. They arranged for books to be sent there. When the library opened, the women took turns working as volunteer librarians.

Life in Jasper was good, but Frank and Ruth felt they wanted more. They wanted a child. A short time later they adopted a baby boy. They named him James

Frank and Ruth with their son, Johnny.

Curtis Johnson, although he would mostly be known as "Johnny."

After the adoption, Ruth resigned her teaching job so she could stay home and take care of the infant. Frank could not wait for him to grow a bit, so he could take him fishing. In later years that would be a favorite pastime for the two of them.

In 1952, Frank got involved in politics, backing Army general Dwight "Ike" Eisenhower for president. Frank had great respect for Ike, who had been the commanding general in the invasion of France. Frank became chairman of the "Alabama Veterans for Ike."

In November 1952, Ike won the election, defeating Democrat Adlai Stephenson. The victory would have a dramatic impact on Frank Johnson's career.

In 1953, Eisenhower named Frank to be the U.S. Attorney for North Alabama. It paid less than he was making as a Jasper lawyer. But he accepted.

"I thought I would take the job for a couple of years and then go back to private practice," he said.

With that in mind, he continued living in Jasper, driving to Birmingham every day to the main office. As U.S. Attorney, he prosecuted bank robbery cases and other federal crimes. In 1954, he handled what has been called "the last slavery case" in the South.

Frank Sikora and Michelle Batcheler

Two white men in Sumter County, Alabama would go into Mississippi and pay the fines of black men who were in jail on minor charges. The white men then made the black men come back to their farm and work out the fine. Often, they would make them stay for several weeks to pay off a $10 debt.

One black man named Monk Thompson decided he had worked long enough and fled the farm. The owners caught him and made him return, where he was beaten with whips. Thompson died.

A black funeral home owner called Frank and reported the death. Frank sent two FBI agents to Sumter County to investigate. After getting their report, Frank charged the brothers with peonage—a type of slavery—and prosecuted them at trial in Birmingham. They were found guilty.

Frank made news as a man who would strictly follow the law, no matter where it led. He would become even better known for that later on.

Chapter 6

IN THE SPRING OF 1955 the elderly federal judge in Montgomery, Charles Kennamer, died. Right away Frank was mentioned as a replacement.

"Every lawyer wants one day to be a judge," he said. "I was no different."

In October 1955 President Eisenhower made it official, choosing Frank to be the federal judge in Montgomery. Frank and his wife and son drove to the Alabama capital on Nov. 7, 1955 for the swearing-in ceremony. He was 37, the youngest federal judge in the United States. He would soon become the best known.

On Dec. 1, 1955, a black woman named Rosa Parks, a tailor's assistant at a Montgomery department store, boarded a bus to go home. But soon a quiet ride home turned into a national news event. The driver stopped the bus and told her to move to the back so a white man could have her seat.

She refused to move. The driver called police and soon two officers came on board and told Mrs. Parks she was under arrest.

Within a few hours, E.D. Nixon, the local president of the National Association for the Advancement of Colored People (NAACP) and Clifford Durr, a white attorney, and his wife, Virginia, were at the jail to get Mrs. Parks released.

Late that night, Nixon said that blacks should refuse to ride the buses in Montgomery to protest their treatment.

Leaflets were printed and handed out in black areas of the city. "Don't ride the bus on Monday," they read.

At churches that Sunday, December 4, ministers passed the word along about the planned boycott.

The arrest of Mrs. Parks was not the first time something like that had happened. In March 1955, a black girl, Claudette Colvin, 15, had been arrested for refusing to give her bus seat to a white man.

The same thing had happened to three other black women. Two of them had obeyed the bus driver; the third was arrested.

On Monday, December 5, the boycott began, with almost 30,000 blacks walking to work or school. The buses rolled empty through the city.

Frank M. Johnson, Jr.: Courageous Judge

At the same time, black people formed a group to lead the boycott. It was called the Montgomery Improvement Association. Chosen as the leader was the young pastor of Dexter Avenue Baptist Church, the Rev. Martin Luther King, Jr. He was only 27.

The church was a block away from the Alabama State Capitol. (Many people noticed that the church was near the place where—nearly a hundred years before—Jefferson Davis was sworn in as president of the Confederacy, shortly before the start of the Civil War.)

As he drove to work in the mornings, Judge Johnson saw the many black people walking. To himself he said, "One day this thing is coming to me."

Sure enough it did.

In February 1956 Fred Gray, one of two black attorneys in Montgomery, filed suit in federal court asking that the state's segregation law be removed.

When a state law is challenged it takes three federal judges to make a decision. Judge Richard Rives and Judge Seybourn Lynne joined Johnson.

The case was heard May 11, 1956. The courtroom was packed. The judges listened as four black people told of being either arrested or made to move from their seats on the buses.

All four—Aurelia Browder, 34, Mary Louise Smith, 19, Susie McDonald, 77, and Claudette Colvin, 15—said they would ride the buses again if there was no segregation.

Miss Colvin's testimony was emotional, and some women in the audience cried. She told about police boarding the bus and saying to her: "Why are you not going to get up? It's against the law here. Aren't you going to get up?"

Said Miss Colvin: "I said, 'No, sir…and I was crying then. I was very hurt because I didn't know white people would act like that. And (the policeman) said, 'I will have to take you off.' So I didn't move. I didn't move at all. So I just acted like a big baby. So he kicked me."

Montgomery Mayor W.A. Gayle said if buses were not segregated, there would be violence.

Other city officials agreed.

The hearing ended that afternoon and all the judges went to Johnson's office. The senior judge, Rives, turned to Johnson and said: "Well, Frank, you're the junior judge here. You vote first. What do you think?"

During the hearing Johnson had not said a word, just listened. But he already had an opinion about the matter.

Frank M. Johnson, Jr.: Courageous Judge

Johnson said, "Judge, as far as I'm concerned, state-imposed segregation violates the Constitution."

Rives nodded, "You know, I feel the same way."

The law that required segregation came from a U.S. Supreme Court decision in 1896. That case, called *Plessy vs. Ferguson,* had challenged segregation in train stations in Louisiana. At that time, the Supreme Court upheld the state law. It led to the practice that black and white people could be kept separate so long as they were treated equally. Lawyers called it "separate but equal."

Johnson and Rives didn't believe that the 1896 decision was correct. In fact, in 1954 the Supreme Court ruled that segregation in schools was illegal. Johnson and Rives felt that if it was illegal to have separate schools for black and white children, then it must be illegal for them to be kept separate in other places.

The two judges spent several days preparing their order. It was made public June 5, 1956. Newspapers headlined the story: Two federal judges had struck down segregation on Montgomery city buses.

The city appealed to the U.S. Supreme Court, but lost.

On a December morning in 1956, Martin Luther

King Jr., Rosa Parks and other black people boarded city buses for the first time in more than a year.

The modern Civil Rights Movement had scored its first victory in Montgomery, Alabama.

For Judge Johnson, it meant a flood of hate mail and angry telephone calls. And one Saturday night as he and Ruth visited some friends, they received a call to return home, that there was a problem.

Rushing back to the house, they found a blazing cross in their front yard.

The fiery cross was the traditional symbol of the Ku Klux Klan (KKK), the white hate group that had terrorized blacks and some whites since the end of the Civil War.

"We didn't let it bother us," Johnson said later. "Ruth is a strong person. She's a Winston County girl."

In other parts of Montgomery, more deadly things happened. Bombs exploded at the homes of some black leaders. One was found

The Ku Klux Klan burned crosses, frightening many citizens.

Frank M. Johnson, Jr.: Courageous Judge

on the front porch of Martin Luther King's home.

Bullets struck some buses, and several black bus riders were wounded. White people who believed in segregation frightened and hurt black people in the coming years, and burning crosses flickered in the night skies across Alabama.

Chapter 7

FRANK JOHNSON KNEW there was a chance he would get threats from the KKK. However, he never dreamed he and a law-school classmate, George C. Wallace, would become bitter rivals about equal rights for black people.

But in 1957, the two found themselves in conflict over black people's right to vote.

It started when the U.S. Civil Rights Commission came to Alabama to look into charges that blacks were denied the right to vote.

Wallace was a state judge for a part of Alabama that included Bullock County, where only five blacks were registered to vote. The Civil Rights Commission asked to see voting records for Bullock and Barbour counties.

Wallace refused, telling them he had locked up the records. Further, he said, "I will arrest any federal agents who try to get them."

The fight for the records came to Frank Johnson's

Frank M. Johnson, Jr.: Courageous Judge

court in Montgomery. The judge ordered Wallace to allow the federal commission to see the voting records. Wallace again refused.

Johnson said he wanted to hear both sides of the argument, and told those involved to be in his courtroom in January 1958. If Wallace did not obey the order, he could be sent to prison. Days passed and the records remained in Wallace's control. He said he would not give them up.

Then, one Sunday night, just before the hearing was to be held, Johnson got a telephone call from a friend who said Wallace wanted to pay him a visit. "Tell him to come on," the judge said. "I'll wait up for him."

Wallace arrived at the judge's home late that night. He told Johnson that he would not turn over the records. Then he asked the judge to find him guilty and give him a short prison term, just a few days. (A few days in jail would make him look like a hero who went to jail to "defend" Alabama).

Johnson said he would not be part of any such scheme.

"George, I shouldn't even be talking to you," he told Wallace. "But if you don't turn those records over, I'm going to pop you hard."

Johnson meant that he would send Wallace to

prison for more than a few days, probably six months. Surprised that Johnson would not go along with his request, Wallace left.

Early the next morning, Wallace turned the records over to local officials in each county, telling them they could do with them as they pleased. The records were quickly given to the federal commission.

In court a few days later, Johnson found that Wallace, his old friend, had obeyed the order, even though it was in a roundabout way. He dismissed the case.

Wallace, he said later, "was playing politics."

After that, Johnson and Wallace did not speak for more than 15 years, and were never friends again.

To Johnson, it seemed likely that there would be more fights with his old classmate over equal rights for black people.

Chapter 8

VOTING RIGHTS FOR BLACK PEOPLE came after the Civil War. Congress passed the 13th and 14th Amendments. These amendments abolished slavery and gave blacks equal protection of the law.

Then it passed the 15th Amendment, which said that a person could not be denied the right to vote because of race.

Over the next 30 years black men were able to vote. (No women, white or black, were allowed to vote until the first part of the 20th Century.)

But in 1901, Alabama passed a new state constitution that denied voting rights to blacks. Some black people tried to register to vote, but white voting officials used different ways to keep them off the list of people who could vote. Those methods included taxes that voters had to pay and tests.

In 1960, the U.S. Department of Justice went to court for the black people in Macon and Bullock counties. Macon County, the home of Tuskegee Institute, had a population of 26,700, of which 22,300 were black. But only 10 percent of them were registered to vote.

Johnson said he would listen to arguments in the case on February 20, 1961. He soon found the evidence showed clearly that the county officials were not letting black people register to vote just because they were black.

One black woman in Tuskegee said she was turned down because she did not know in which ward, or voting district, she lived. "Since I had never voted before," she said, "I didn't know which ward I was in, even though I lived in the same house for 31 years."

Another black woman said she had lived at the same place "since 1915." The officials said the answer was wrong. Records showed she lived there since "October 30, 1915." She was not allowed to add the month and day to her answer and was rejected.

Even without such cases, Johnson suspected that the officials who signed up voters were not behaving properly. A number of the blacks who had been turned down had college degrees. One of them, William Bailey Hill, had a master's degree from Cornell University and a doctorate from the University of Wisconsin. Yet, he was rejected.

Frank M. Johnson, Jr.: Courageous Judge

On the surface, the blacks were not rejected due to their race, but because they could not pass the tests that voter registrars had created. The people who made up the tests could also make up the rules about what had to be done to pass the tests.

On March 17, 1961, Johnson made his decision. It said the evidence was "overwhelming" that the State of Alabama had kept qualified blacks off the voting rolls. He added, "The discrimination …has been so effective that many have been unable to qualify, while many whites, who have not even finished grammar school, have been registered."

But the order did not cover all Alabama counties, and the struggle by blacks for their right to vote would come before him again.

Chapter 9

THE YEAR 1961 was a time of both unhappiness and celebration in Alabama. It was the 100-year anniversary of the start of the Civil War. Some saw a link between that war and the resistance of many whites to the Civil Rights Movement.

On May 20, 1961, a sunny and warm Saturday, Frank Johnson gathered his fishing gear and looked forward to a peaceful day on Lake Martin, about 30 miles north of Montgomery.

He and Ruth had purchased a cabin there and liked to spend weekends by the water, away from the city. Their son, Johnny, who was then almost 14, had become a fisherman like his dad. He also enjoyed swimming and water skiing.

It had not been a tranquil week in Alabama. The Sunday before, May 14, Mothers Day, a group of college students, mostly black and a few whites, had traveled by bus into Alabama to see if bus stations were still segregated.

Frank M. Johnson, Jr.: Courageous Judge

Earlier, the Department of Commerce had said that bus stations should be open to all passengers, black and white.

The students called themselves Freedom Riders. They rode through Virginia, the Carolinas and Georgia without problems, using both Greyhound and Trailways buses.

They reached the city of Anniston in the early afternoon. As the Trailways bus pulled into the station, a jeering crowd of white men began throwing objects at the vehicle and daring the riders to get off. Police cleared a lane and the driver quickly left the station.

Meantime, the Greyhound bus stopped long enough to see that the Anniston station was closed. It hurried away, again with police help.

However, a long string of cars followed the bus along U.S. 78, the two-lane highway to Birmingham. (The interstate system in Alabama was not yet complete.)

A few miles out of the city a tire on the bus blew out—some believed it had been hit by a gunshot—and it limped to a halt alongside the road.

Quickly, a mob surrounded it and began shouting ugly things to the riders. Then someone threw something that broke a window and then caught fire. Smoke poured out the windows and soon the bus was on fire.

Shouting in terror and choking for breath, the Freedom Riders stumbled out of the burning bus, only to be attacked by the white men just outside.

The students were in trouble, and were desperate to find help. Just then an Alabama Highway Patrolman arrived. He drew his gun and fired a shot into the air, shouting at the white men to leave.

About the same time, the Trailways bus arrived in Birmingham where members of the KKK attacked the riders as they got off the bus.

In Washington, President John Kennedy urged Alabama Gov. John Patterson to assure the safety of all travelers. The governor said he could not protect everyone.

President Kennedy and Attorney General Robert Kennedy asked the Freedom Riders to stop their ride for a while to let everything cool down. But the Freedom Riders vowed to continue their journey.

On May 20, the Saturday that Judge Johnson was fishing, the Freedom Riders arrived at the Greyhound station in Montgomery. A mob of about 1,000 surrounded the bus.

When the Freedom Riders got off the bus, white men attacked them with clubs. Most were believed to be members of the KKK. Montgomery police officers

Frank M. Johnson, Jr.: Courageous Judge

stood around doing nothing or directed traffic.

By then a black student, William Barbee, had been hit by a man with a bat and knocked to the pavement. The crowd shouted, "Kill him! Kill him!"

Rushing to the site, Floyd Mann, the Alabama director of Public Safety, led state troopers into the crowd. Firing several shots into the air, he ordered the mob to retreat.

He saved Barbee's life. Also rescued was John Seigenthaler, an advisor to President Kennedy who had been sent to Montgomery to see what was going on. He was knocked out.

That evening as Judge Johnson prepared to fry some fish he had caught, a boat pulled up to his dock. In it was John Doar of the U.S. Justice Department. A U.S. Marshal was with him.

Doar asked Johnson to issue an order that would stop the KKK from attacking the students.

At that moment, the Freedom Riders and 800 blacks, including Martin Luther King Jr., were in the black First Baptist Church, about three blocks from the Alabama State Capitol. An angry mob of 2,000 whites surrounded the church, throwing stones and breaking windows. As the night wore on, several cars were set on fire.

President Kennedy ordered 400 U.S. Marshals to

Montgomery. They joined Mann's 200 state troopers at the church. The situation grew more dangerous by the minute as the mob threatened to rush the church and go inside.

Finally, Governor Patterson ordered the Alabama National Guard to the church. The troops arrived with bayonets on their rifles. The angry mob of white people began to drift away.

Monday morning, Judge Johnson set a hearing for May 29. The defendants in the case were members of the KKK, Montgomery Police Commissioner L.B. Sullivan, and other Montgomery and Birmingham officials.

Frank M. Johnson, Jr.: Courageous Judge

Chapter 10

THE FIRST WITNESS was Patricia Jenkins, 19, a student at Tennessee A&I University in Nashville. She testified about the morning of May 20 when the Greyhound bus pulled into the station in Montgomery.

She recalled the words of the bus driver, who said, "This is Montgomery. And these are the Freedom Riders, the tamers of the South."

"The what of the South?" a defense attorney asked.

"The tamers," she replied.

"Go over that again," said Judge Johnson. "The bus driver said that?"

"Yes, he did," she said. "The tamers of the South."

Miss Jenkins then told about the crowd of whites that had gathered quickly. One man, who wore a white shirt and had a cigar in his mouth, began hitting a news photographer, she said.

"Well, these people began to follow this man, and a lot of people began to jump on (the photographer) and—"

"Lot of people began to what?" a defense attorney cut in.

"They jumped on him," she said. "You know,

Frank M. Johnson as federal judge.

jumped on him."

There was some laughter in the spectator section. She then told about the students being attacked by the mob, and having cameras smashed and suitcases thrown about.

Her testimony brought more whispers and laughter from spectators.

A defense attorney, Clarence Atkeison, questioned Miss Jenkins.

"Now all of you on the bus had discussed the trip many times, had you not?"

"Yes we had."

"And you planned it with each other, hadn't you?"

"Planned it?" she asked. "What do you mean, 'planned'?"

"Well, you're a college student," Atkeison drawled. "You know what 'planning' means, don't you?"

There was more laughter in the spectator section.

Judge Johnson raised a hand to the attorney. "All right, Mr. Atkeison," he said.

The judge then peered over his half-rim glasses at the audience.

"That just brings me to the point that has been arriving ever since we started this case." There was silence. Johnson, his voice frosty, went on: "You people that came here for the purpose of expressing hilarity and frivolity, you are going to stop it or I am going to exclude you from the courtroom. That is the last time I am going to mention it." He meant that they were not to laugh any more.

He told the U.S. Marshals in the courtroom to remove anyone who violated the order.

One thing Judge Johnson would not stand for was disrespect in the courtroom. "It's not for me," he once said. "It's respect for the court and what the law means in this country."

As the Freedom Riders case went on, there was no more laughter from the audience.

The judge also demanded respect for the witnesses. Several times in the Freedom Riders case he had to remind attorneys to be respectful.

Once, a defense attorney, in questioning Miss Jenkins, drew the judge's stern comment when he asked: "Patricia, you say you saw the man with the camera pointing his camera in the face of the man with the cigar?"

"I didn't say that," she replied. "I said—"

The attorney interrupted. "You just got through saying—"

"Wait a minute," said the judge. "Don't argue with the witness. You question her properly. Don't argue with her."

"Thank you, sir," said the attorney.

William Barbee, the student who had been severely beaten, testified that he had been knocked down "by three gentlemen."

Defense attorney Calvin Whitesell inquired, "Did he say 'three gentlemen', your honor?"

"That's what he said," Johnson shot back.

Chapter 11

AMONG THE WITNESSES were members of the Ku Klux Klan, some of whom had taken part in the beatings. All tried not to answer questions.

Typical was the testimony of Robert Shelton of Tuscaloosa, the leader, or Imperial Wizard, of the KKK. John Doar of the Justice Department questioned him: "How long were you an officer in the Knights of the Ku Klux Klan?"

"I don't remember."

"Other than yourself, who are the executive officers of the organization?" Doar asked.

"They are listed on the charter, sir," Shelton replied.

"Does the Alabama Knights have any local klaverns?" Doar asked. (A klavern is a local KKK unit.)

"Beg your pardon?"

Doar later asked if Shelton knew any KKK members personally.

"I do not have any records," he said, "to verify the

fact that any individuals are members of the Alabama Knights."

"That is not responsive to the question," the judge injected. "Ask the question again, Mr. Doar."

Doar repeated the question.

"To authenticate it, I do not," Shelton said.

"That is not responsive," Johnson snapped. "Read the question again."

Finally Shelton said, "Those on the charter are the only ones I am familiar with."

After several more minutes of questioning, Johnson called a recess.

The Klansman's attorney, James Hammonds, quickly stood up and said, "May I speak to you, your honor?"

"I'll talk to you during the recess," the judge replied. "And let me state this as a matter of record. During this recess I suggest you talk to Mr. Shelton about his evasiveness on the questions."

"That was my idea for taking a recess," Hammonds said.

"Yes, sir," said the judge, his voice sharp. "I suggest you take advantage of this recess to do that, because I don't want to put Mr. Shelton in jail until he has been advised by his lawyer."

After the recess, Shelton looked up at the judge

and said, "Your honor, I'd like to reconsider some of my answers."

"All right," Johnson said.

Facing the threat of jail, Shelton had better answers to the questions.

At the end of the hearing, Judge Johnson issued an order against the KKK, the Montgomery police as well as the civil rights groups that sponsored the Freedom Riders.

His order charged that the Montgomery Police Department and its leaders "willfully and deliberately failed to take measures to ensure the safety of the students and to prevent unlawful acts of violence by the KKK upon them."

While the order said that the KKK caused the violence and the police allowed it, the order also targeted the Freedom Riders and their sponsors, saying that the trouble their presence drew in Alabama was "an undue burden upon the free flow of interstate commerce."

It added, "The fact that this agitation on the part of the (Freedom Riders) is within the law…the right of the public to be protected from the evils of their conduct is a greater and more important right."

"Now gentlemen," he said, before handing out copies of the order, "if there are other such occurrences...I am going to put some Klansmen, some city officials, and some policemen and some Negro preachers in the U.S. Penitentiary in Atlanta, Georgia. And that is all I am going to say about it."

Chapter 12

IN 1962 GEORGE WALLACE WAS ELECTED governor of Alabama. While he was running for governor, he called Judge Johnson a "carpetbaggin', scalawaggin' liar."

Wallace's fiery words inspired some of the people to send hateful letters to Johnson. Others called the judge and threatened him over the telephone. The judge shrugged them off, telling friends he would not allow words to bother him.

In January 1963, Wallace was sworn in as governor. On that cold day, he made a famous speech in which he said there would be "segregation forever" in Alabama, meaning that he would do everything he could to keep black people and white people separated from each other. It was not long before he put those words into action.

In June 1963, when two black people tried to register as students at the University of Alabama, Wallace promised to "stand in the schoolhouse door" to keep them out. Hundreds of people gathered at the University's Foster Auditorium to see the standoff. State troopers and National Guard soldiers stood by. In the end, Wallace failed and he stepped aside to allow Vivian Malone and James Hood to go inside and register.

Next, the school battle moved to Judge Johnson's court. Attorneys in the town of Tuskegee sued to have all-white Tuskegee High School admit black students. Johnson ordered the school to let in the 13 black students who had applied for admission.

All seemed to be worked out, and parents in Tuskegee held meetings to ensure an orderly start of school in early September.

But the night before classes were to begin, Governor Wallace sent dozens of state troopers to Tuskegee. When students arrived the next morning, troopers stood in front of the school, blocking the entrances.

"The school is closed," a trooper told the students. "Go home."

When Judge Johnson was told what happened, he quickly set a hearing. He ordered the high school to admit the black students. School officials did so, but soon all of the white students left and enrolled in a private school.

For a time Tuskegee High was open with only the 13 black students. After Christmas vacation, the school did not re-open. Officials said it was too expensive to hold classes for such a small number.

Johnson then ordered the students to be admitted at the high school in Notasulga, five miles away. But the same thing happened there. All the whites left.

Six of the black students were the only ones at Notasulga; the others attended classes at the nearby community of Shorter. At Notasulga, part of the school was burned. But classes continued.

One morning in May 1964, the worried principal said graduation would be held that day within an hour. There was no time to send out invitations, or even to notify parents. Three black students were the only ones in the graduation class. They stood on the stage and sang "No Man Is An Island," and then were given their diplomas. The ceremony was over.

The school problems just wouldn't go away. In 1967, Johnson and four other federal judges ordered schools all over Alabama to allow black and white students to attend the same schools. After that, most Alabama school systems opened to all students, regardless of race.

Frank M. Johnson, Jr.: Courageous Judge

Chapter 13

THE CIVIL RIGHTS MOVEMENT in the South—a fight for black people to have the same rights as white people—made people so angry that sometimes, some of them did mean things that hurt or killed other people. In September 1963 four black girls were killed when a bomb exploded at the Sixteenth Street Baptist Church in Birmingham. In June 1964, three civil rights workers—two whites and one black—were murdered near Philadelphia, Miss. These were dangerous times.

By 1965, the eye of the Civil Rights Movement was fixed on Selma, Alabama. The Baptist preacher and civil rights leader Martin Luther King Jr., spoke there on January 2. He said that he would help black people there and in other rural Alabama counties get the right to vote.

That area is known as the Black Belt. It is rolling prairie land where fields of cotton stretch into a horizon of crooked fences, aging shanties and sprawling plantation homes.

The name Black Belt came for two reasons: One, the soil is rich and black, good for growing cotton. Second, black people made up a lot of the population. They were the descendants of slaves who had worked the land a century earlier.

Dallas County, where Selma is located, had over 25,000 black people. But only 300 were registered to vote. In Wilcox and Lowndes counties, which were right next to Dallas County, not one black person was registered to vote.

A federal judge in Mobile had ordered voting officials in Selma to open the registrar's office two days a month and register 100 black people each day. That would be 200 people a month. At that rate, it would take years to register all of the black people who were old enough to vote.

Martin Luther King said it was not enough. So he led a series of marches in Selma. Each day he marched, Sheriff Jim Clark met him and the marchers, and often arrested hundreds of people, including children.

Judge Johnson read and watched news reports of what was going on in Selma.

Then, on February 18, black people planned a night march in Marion, Alabama, 28 miles west of Selma.

Frank M. Johnson, Jr.: Courageous Judge

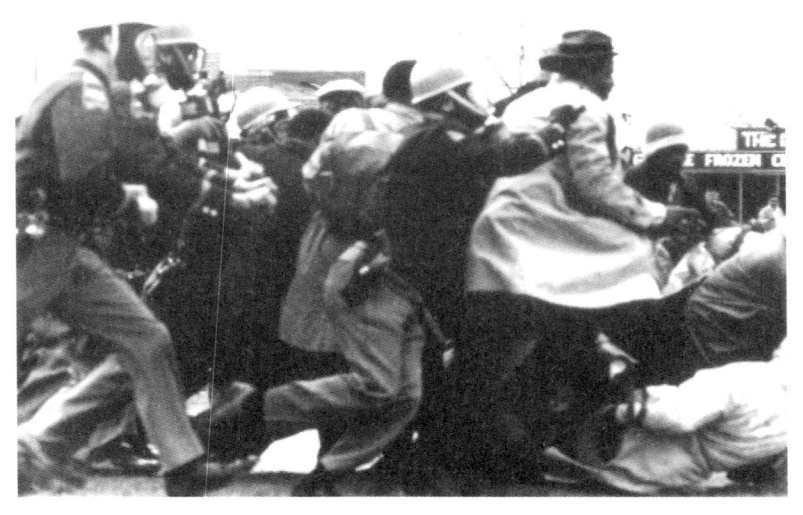

Officers chase civil rights marchers.

As the black people came out of a church to begin a short march to the county jail, someone fired shots and the streetlights went out. In the darkness there were shouts. Some white men sprayed black paint on the cameras of newsmen. One news reporter was beaten.

About 400 people began the march. Then Alabama State Troopers stopped them and the night erupted with the sound of screams and the *thud-thud-thud* of clubs striking bodies. The people panicked. They ran and troopers chased them. Then a trooper fired a shot. It struck a black man, Jimmie Lee Jackson. He died a week later.

Some of the black leaders called for a march from

Selma to Montgomery to protest to Governor Wallace for voting rights and against police brutality. Wallace warned that such a march would not be allowed.

In spite of the warning, the marchers started the journey on the afternoon of March 7, 1965. About 600 blacks and some whites walked through downtown Selma to the Edmund Pettus Bridge, which spans the Alabama River. Beyond was U.S. 80, the road to Montgomery.

A line of Alabama State Troopers dressed in their blue uniforms waited across the bridge. As the marchers stopped and asked if they could say a prayer, the lawmen slammed into them, swinging clubs and rolling canisters of tear gas into the crowd of marchers, stinging their eyes.

Behind the troopers came a group of sheriff's deputies on horseback. Charging forward, they flailed the marchers with clubs and whips.

One black girl, Sheyann Webb, who was nine on that Sunday, said she later had nightmares about being chased by masked men on horses who rode through the rising clouds of gas.

In all, about 80 people were hurt, including John Lewis, who, in 1961, had been beaten as a Freedom Rider.

On Monday morning, March 8, attorneys for the

marchers and the U.S. government, went to Johnson's office and filed suit against Governor Wallace and Selma officials. The marchers asked for an order from the judge that would allow them to march from Selma to Montgomery without being stopped by Wallace's lawmen.

In Selma, hundreds of black people stood outside Brown Chapel AME Church and sang freedom songs, such as "We Shall Overcome," the anthem of the Civil Rights Movement.

Meanwhile, dozens of ministers and others came to Selma to join the march. On the night of March 9 a church minister, James Reeb, 38, of Boston, was attacked by several white men who hit him with a ball bat. He was rushed to University Hospital in Birmingham where he went into a coma and later died.

Selma was no longer just a place. It was a national story and also, *Newsweek* magazine said, a "state of mind." Every major news source in the nation came to Alabama to cover the story.

Johnson began the hearing on March 11. Martin Luther King, Jr., testified about the need to walk instead of driving to Montgomery. Attorney Jack Greenberg asked about the planning that had been made for the March 7 event.

"Well, the plan was to engage in a peaceful, nonviolent walk from Selma to Montgomery," King replied, "where we would present a petition to Governor Wallace protesting the denial of the right to vote and the tragic and terrible police brutality that we had experienced in Selma."

"Why had you planned to walk…?"

"First, we were dealing with the whole question of poverty in the Negro community," King said. "The vast majority cannot afford an automobile. (We) had to dramatize the condition of poverty, and to engage in the kind of self-inflicted suffering that would be involved in walking fifty miles to call attention to the evils and the injustices that we were facing in Alabama."

Earlier King was harshly questioned by an attorney for the state and Judge Johnson sharply called him down. Now, that same state attorney, John Kohn, questioned another black leader, Rev. F.D. Reese of Selma. Johnson would again show that he demanded fairness from the attorneys.

"Besides being president of the Dallas Voter League, what else do you do?" Kohn asked.

"I'm a teacher," Reese replied.

"Are you on anybody's payroll paying you to agitate?" Kohn asked.

"Object," a government attorney called.

"I'm cross-examining him," Kohn snapped.

Judge Johnson quickly reminded Kohn, "You came into this case late, too, with the court's permission."

Kohn nodded. "Yes sir."

Johnson stared at Kohn. "It has been necessary during this trial for me to advise (the lawyers) that when they examine they are to show common courtesy to all of these witnesses, regardless of who they are or what color they are."

Some of the witnesses had been marchers who were at the bridge and told of being struck with clubs and whips, being temporarily blinded by tear gas, and chased by horsemen.

Then Col. Al Lingo, the Alabama director of Public Safety, was called to the witness stand. He told of ordering the troopers to disperse the marchers who had paused at the end of the bridge.

Attorney Fred Gray cross-examined: "Regarding your orders to halt the march: who gave the order?"

"I got them from the governor," Lingo replied.

"And what did he instruct you to do?" Gray asked.

"He did not instruct me," Lingo said. "He just said there would be no march."

"Regardless?" Judge Johnson interrupted. To Gray,

he said, "Just a minute." Then back to Lingo: "Regardless what it took to do it?"

Lingo shook his head, "Well, I don't mean to kill any of them, but to use the means of least force as possible to restrain them—"

"But whatever it took to do it?" Johnson asked.

"Yes sir."

"Regardless of what it was?"

"No sir. Not regardless."

Johnson stared at him for a moment. Then: "Where were you going to stop, Colonel?"

Chapter 14

ON MONDAY NIGHT, March 15, 1965, President Lyndon Johnson spoke on television to the nation about Selma and the right to vote.

The president said, "At times history and fate meet at a single time in a single place to shape a turning point in man's unending search for freedom. So it was at Lexington and Concord. So it was last week in Selma, Alabama.

"The efforts of American Negroes to secure for themselves the full blessings of American life must be our cause, too," the president said. "Because it is not just Negroes, but really it is all of us who must overcome the crippling legacy of bigotry and injustice."

After a pause, he slowly declared, "And we shall overcome."

Martin Luther King Jr., was watching the speech at a home in Selma. When the president used the title of the freedom song, those nearby said tears rolled down King's face.

Meanwhile, after another day of the hearing, Judge Frank Johnson went to his office and prepared to write his order. While he felt all cases before him were important, he knew this one was being watched by millions of Americans as well as people in other nations.

The issue was the right of people to peacefully get together and march along a major highway that was used by thousands of motorists. That right is contained in the first paragraph of the U.S. Constitution.

Judge Johnson knew the decision was his alone to make. On his desk was a glass paperweight that contained words that he always relied on. They were the words of Abraham Lincoln:

I do the very best I know how, the very best I can and mean to keep doing so until the end. If the end brings me out all right, what is said against me won't amount to anything. If the end brings me out wrong, ten angels swearing I was right would make no difference.

On Wednesday March 17, 1965, Johnson issued his order. The march from Selma to Montgomery could be held.

President Johnson assured him that the government would protect the marchers. (Lyndon Johnson told some politicians and news reporters, "I wouldn't have to be president if my name was *Frank* Johnson.")

When the judge's order was read to the people who had gathered at Brown Chapel AME Church in Selma, a mighty cheer arose. By then there were more than a thousand there.

Judge Johnson's order stated that law enforcement officers had mistreated black people in Selma. Those officers, the order said, were "not enforcing any valid law of the State of Alabama."

It continued: "(It) seems basic to our constitutional principles that the extent of the right to assemble…and march peaceably along the highways and streets in an orderly manner should be (weighed against) the enormity of the wrongs that are being protested…. In this case, the wrongs are enormous."

In conclusion, the order read: "It is recognized that the plan reaches to the outer limits of what is constitutionally allowed. However, the wrongs and injustices inflicted upon these plaintiffs have clearly exceeded what is constitutionally permissible."

On March 21, a Sunday, King led 4,000 marchers across the Edmund Pettus Bridge and onto U.S. 80 to start the journey to Montgomery. This time, there were no state troopers to stop them. The Alabama National Guard had been placed on duty and soldiers walked in front and beside the marchers to protect them. Soldiers in jeeps and other military vehicles rode ahead to assure there were no snipers along the roadside. Helicopters hovered overhead. In addition, President Johnson ordered 1,000 Army paratroopers to be stationed nearby in case of trouble.

After several miles, the march dwindled to 300 who were chosen to walk the entire fifty miles. At night they camped along the road, using land offered by people who supported the march.

The group arrived in Montgomery on March 24 in a driving rain. That night they camped on the grounds of The City of St. Jude, a Catholic school and charity center on the outskirts of the city. A concert was held featuring recording stars and some movie actors. Among them were Burt Lancaster, Harry Belafonte, Tony Bennett, the group Peter, Paul and Mary, and Sammy Davis, Jr.

In the late morning of March 25, the marchers headed for the Alabama Capitol. Judge Johnson watched from a window in the United States Courthouse. He had never seen a demonstration before. Later he would say, "If I was a black person, I might have been in the march."

There, in the afternoon, King spoke to the cheers of more than 10,000. On the outskirts of the crowd were some members of the KKK. They said ugly things to those watching and listening to King. Despite all the troops and the FBI agents, trouble was brewing.

That night, as marchers returned to Selma, a white woman from Detroit, Mrs. Viola Liuzzo, 38, was shot and killed. She was driving her car to Montgomery to pick up some of the marchers. The shooting happened in Lowndes County.

A day later, the FBI arrested three members of the KKK—Collie Leroy Wilkins, Eugene Thomas, and W.O. Eaton. They had followed Mrs. Liuzzo that night. The fatal shots were fired as they passed her car.

The march had drawn the attention of all America to the problem of voting rights being denied to blacks. The protests in Selma and the march to Montgomery led to passage of the Voting Rights Act of 1965. President Johnson signed it on August 6 of that year.

It not only gave black people the right to be registered, but also allowed the federal government to send agents to the South to make sure that they were signed up. Thousands of black people in rural counties lined up to become voters.

One of them was Janie Belle Gibbs of Marion, who was 93. Later she said, "I would run to the courthouse if I could."

Johnson's order prompted dozens of letters and phone calls to his office. While some were threatening, many were supportive. One letter, even with its misspelled words, had an important message:

Dear Mr. Johnson: I think you are a vary good judge. I am not Negro, but I do believe the Negros deserve freedom. Here is my picture and here is my address. I am 8 years old and I appreciate what you are doing for our great country.

Love, Dawn Bennett,
San Diego, Calif.

Chapter 15

THE MEN CHARGED with the murder of Mrs. Liuzzo were found not guilty in a Lowndes County trial. But they were not yet free.

The federal government charged them with conspiracy to violate Mrs. Liuzzo's civil rights. In December 1965, that trial was held before Judge Johnson. The Klansmen had not known that a fourth man in the car, Gary Thomas Rowe, was an FBI informant.

After hearing 40 witnesses, Judge Johnson explained to the jury about the law involved in the case. He reminded them that part of the case was based on "circumstantial evidence."

To help them with that term, he said, "If it snows during the night and you get up the next morning and see rabbit tracks going by your door, you know that a rabbit went by, even though you did not see him."

The jury argued about the case, but they couldn't come to a decision. So they then returned to the courtroom.

Johnson told them, "You have not begun to deliberate long enough to say you are hopelessly deadlocked." He urged them to continue. "It is very desirable that you jurors should agree upon a verdict." An hour later they returned. All three men were found guilty.

Johnson spoke to the jurors: "Gentlemen, if it's worth anything to you, in my opinion that was the only verdict that you could possibly reach in this case and still reach a fair and honest and just verdict."

He sentenced the Klansmen to ten years in prison, the maximum allowed by law. Wilkins and Thomas served seven years each. Eaton died before beginning his sentence.

Frank M. Johnson, Jr.: Courageous Judge

Chapter 16

ON THE NIGHT OF APRIL 25, 1967, the years of threats made against Judge Johnson came true. A bomb exploded at the home of his mother, Alabama Long Johnson. She had just left the kitchen and gone upstairs to go to bed when the bomb exploded. The judge and the FBI knew that it was meant for him.

Johnson's parents had moved to Montgomery in the mid-1940s when his father took a job with the Veterans Administration. Their telephone was listed as Frank M. Johnson, the same as Judge Johnson. Mr. Johnson had died in 1965.

"I had an unlisted number," Judge Johnson said. "Mother, who lived alone, kept the same number that was in the phone book. Whoever put the bomb there thought it was my house."

The explosion did not injure his mother, but damaged the house badly. Had Mrs. Johnson been in the living room she surely would have been seriously injured or even killed.

(Some believe the years of threats bothered Johnny Johnson so much that in 1975, at age 26, he took his own life.)

Angered by the bombing, Judge Johnson hurried to his mother's home and borrowed a flashlight from one of the firemen. Then he prowled about in the darkness, looking through the debris. Later he admitted, "I didn't know what I was looking for. I was just looking."

Finally, he gave the flashlight back and talked to the FBI agents. They assured him that they would keep some agents there and watch the house. They remained there for several days and nights. Then Mrs. Johnson asked them to leave. She insisted on staying in her home.

Over the years, some of the hatred for Judge Johnson began to fade away. Eventually, the U.S. marshals who stood guard at his house at night were removed. Life became more orderly and normal.
In the early 1990s, a man told the FBI agents that he had placed the bomb at Mrs. Johnson's home that night in 1967. The man, Thomas Tarrants III, said he drove from Mobile to Montgomery and looked up the address in the telephone book. He said he assumed it was the judge's house. In his statement, he said he did not intend to injure anyone.

Chapter 17

JUDGE JOHNSON SELDOM TOOK the problems of his court cases home with him. On weekends he spent hours making grandfather clocks or building cabinets of cherry wood. Most of these he gave as gifts to friends and family members. He also was proud of growing roses.

But his favorite hobby was fishing. And when he fished, he liked to catch more than anyone else.

Two friends went with him one night. Both men began catching fish quickly, but Johnson was unable to land even one. As the night wore on, the two became tired. They wanted to go back to the cabin and sleep. But Johnson insisted on staying on the water. Finally one whispered to the other, "Don't put any bait on your hook. Let him catch up."

That's what they did. Over the next two hours they, of course, did not get a bite. But Johnson finally reeled in about a dozen, putting him ahead.

"Okay, let's go in," he said.

Judge Johnson displays redfish that he caught, and a shark bit off.

The two sleepy friends readily agreed. By then the sun was rising. Instead of getting to sleep, they spent hours cleaning fish.

When Frank and Ruth were first married, he took her fishing with him. He could not get a bite, but she reeled in six in a row. Each time he baited her hook, she hauled in another fish. After her sixth catch, she asked him to bait her hook. In mock anger, Johnson snapped, "Bait your own hook."

Not all of his fishing trips were so peaceful. Once

Frank M. Johnson, Jr.: Courageous Judge

when he was fishing in the Gulf of Mexico, the judge and some friends marveled at a large redfish that he hooked. As the boat bounced about on the choppy Gulf waters, Johnson struggled to get the fish on board.

Just as he was about to reach out and bring it in, there was a sudden splash and a huge grayish object bolted up out of the water and snapped at the dangling redfish. Half of it disappeared before Johnson's eyes. A 10-foot shark had helped himself to a free meal—and shocked the fishermen in the process.

In addition to fishing, Johnson liked to listen to music. His favorite was bluegrass. "All hillbillies like it," he said. He and Mrs. Johnson enjoyed buck dancing as well as waltzes. He also liked to chew tobacco, and sometimes that caused a problem if he was in a public place.

Once, when they were invited to the White House, he and Mrs. Johnson joined the crowd in a waltz. At the start of the dance he had crammed a wad of tobacco into his mouth. As they glided across the room, Johnson managed to whirl her toward the balcony where he quickly spit over the side into some shrubbery.

Chapter 18

EVER SINCE HE WAS A BOY, religion was important to Frank Johnson. In Haleyville, his father had been a deacon at the First Baptist Church. Frank and his brothers and sisters went to church every Sunday and every Wednesday night.

As a judge, Johnson did not bring his religious beliefs into the courtroom, but he did pray privately. "I didn't go to the window and ask God how I should decide a case." He said if God did talk to him about a case, he would be told, "You're the one drawing the judge's salary. You make the decision."

In their earlier years, while still living in Jasper, Frank and Ruth Johnson drove up to Winston County one Sunday afternoon. They stopped at a church where there was a sacred harp singing.

Johnson was so moved by the music that he stood, and to Mrs. Johnson's dismay, asked if he could join in a number. The group not only invited him to take part, but also offered to let him lead. The hymn chosen was "Amazing Grace."

"It was the longest and the worst version of it I ever heard," said Mrs. Johnson, talking about it years later. "I was so embarrassed. I thought it would never end. But Frank was so happy and so pleased with himself."

Not all of Johnson's cases involved big civil rights issues. And even though he was a tough judge, he also had sympathy for people who suffered bad luck and hard times. In one case three men were charged with stealing food from a government warehouse.

Two of the men, who were black, pleaded guilty. The third man, who was white, said he was innocent. A trial was held and a jury found the white man not guilty.

Johnson felt it was wrong to sentence the two blacks to prison when the white man, who was the ringleader, got off free. So he called the two black men up to him for sentencing. He sentenced each to spend 30 minutes in the presence of a U.S. Marshal.

Another time a young white man was convicted of stealing property from a government building. He could have been sentenced to several years in prison. But Johnson noticed a young woman sitting in the courtroom holding a baby.

As the young man stood before him, the judge asked: "Who is the girl with the baby?"

"That's my girl friend and our baby, judge," the man replied.

Johnson leaned forward. "You come back in two weeks for sentencing. If you bring your girl friend with you, she can watch as I send you to prison. But if you bring your *wife*, I will put you on two years of probation."

"Yes, sir, judge. Thank you."

The man got the message. He and the girl were married in a few days and when he returned, he was given probation, which meant he did not have to go to prison.

Over the years, some of Johnson's cases were amusing, to say the least. In one of them, when he was a judge on the 11th Circuit Court of Appeals, based in Atlanta, he actually heard a case about a talking cat. Yes, the owners of the cat said it could talk. Even a federal judge in Georgia said he heard the cat purr, "I love you."

The issue was not whether the animal—named Blackie—could speak, but if his owners should have to pay a license fee to the city of Augusta, Georgia.

Frank M. Johnson, Jr.: Courageous Judge

The city claimed that the cat's owners, Carl and Elaine Miles, stood on the street and people paid them to hear the cat talk. The city said they should have to buy a business license. Mr. and Mrs. Miles said they should not, because they did not charge. They said people merely donated money.

Johnson wrote that he and two other judges had to disagree with the argument of Mr. and Mrs. Miles.

They had to buy a business license. Johnson wrote that Blackie was not covered by the free speech clause of the law, because he was not a person. Besides, Judge Johnson said in his opinion, Mr. and Mrs. Miles had no need to file suit on the cat's behalf, because, as he wrote, "Blackie can clearly speak for himself."

Chapter 19

BY THE 1990s Judge Johnson knew his career was winding down. Looking back at the trials he presided over, it was clear the one that was in the spotlight was the Selma-to-Montgomery trial. That case, and the events that swirled around it, led to passage of the Voting Rights Act of 1965.

The impact was extremely important. In 1960 there were 53,336 black voters in Alabama. By 1990, the number had swelled to 537,285.

"The Civil Rights Movement," he said, "was a social and legal revolution. The causes were the same ones that led to the Civil War."

Even before he retired, his fellow judges and other important people from all across the country honored Judge Johnson.

A number of colleges and universities gave him honorary doctorate degrees. They included Notre Dame, Princeton, Yale, the University of Alabama, Mississippi State University, Montevallo University,

Frank M. Johnson, Jr.: Courageous Judge

Birmingham-Southern College, Boston University, Tuskegee University, St. Michael's College, and New York University.

In 1992, the federal government renamed the United States Courthouse in Montgomery to the Frank M. Johnson Jr. Federal Building and United States Courthouse. At the ceremony, a band played "The Battle Hymn of the Republic." Johnson made a short speech in which he cited the words of President Abraham Lincoln.

I do the very best I know how, the very best I can and mean to keep doing so until the end. If the end brings me out all right, what is said against me won't amount to anything.

In 1995, President Bill Clinton named Johnson as recipient of the Presidential Medal of Freedom, the highest award given to a civilian.

Clinton said that in Johnson's 40 years on the bench, the judge's "landmark decisions in the areas of desegregation, voting rights and civil liberties transformed our understanding of the Constitution."

On November 12, 1996, Clinton signed into law the stretch of U.S. 80 as the "Selma-to-Montgomery National Historic Trail." The 54-mile Voting Rights Trail has museums, parks, wayside panels, walking trails, and other historical markers.

Frank Johnson brought equality to about every phase of life in Alabama to all: parks, the YMCA, and jobs in Alabama government. Blacks could be hired as secretaries, technicians, supervisors, and other white-collar jobs. He ordered the Alabama State Troopers to hire black officers. Within a few years, Alabama had more black troopers than most other states, including many in the North.

And in a decision that he believed was his most important, he ordered Alabama to provide proper care for the mentally ill. Many people who were in mental hospitals, he ruled, were not mental patients at all, but merely elderly citizens who should have been in nursing homes, not mental wards

His legacy is rooted in his belief that the Constitution applies to all Americans. "The strength of the Constitution lies in its flexibility, and its need to change and respond to the special needs of society at a particular time," he said.

His place in history is also forged in the high esteem in which his fellow judges regard him. When he was nominated for a judiciary award, the words of support poured in from other federal judges.

Judge Robert Vance, who lived in the Birmingham area, wrote, "Frank Johnson…is a living monument to the strength and vitality of the Constitution…"

Frank M. Johnson, Jr.: Courageous Judge

Supreme Court Justice William Brennan declared, "I am proud to count Frank Johnson as my friend. I cannot imagine the state of our civil liberties without him."

And U.S. District Judge Foy Guin Jr., wrote, "No more courageous judge ever lived. To honor Frank Johnson is to honor the entire federal judiciary, for he exemplifies its ideals."

Chapter 20

ON A SUMMER DAY IN 1995, Frank and Ruth Johnson drove the 200 miles from Montgomery to their hometown of Haleyville, Alabama, where they had gone to school together so long before.

The occasion was an honor given to Judge Johnson by the town. A plaque was placed in front of the city hall.

The judge smiled shyly as local officials said words of praise about his career as one of the most famous judges in America—if not the most famous. Ruth smiled and tugged at the sleeve of his dark suit.

For all the honors he had received in his years on the bench, this one in his hometown beat them all, he said.

"It means a lot to a fellow when his hometown thinks so well of him," he said to a friend.

He and Ruth had driven around the town before coming to the city hall. Things had changed over the years, he said. The old house that had been his boy-

Frank M. Johnson, Jr.: Courageous Judge

Frank and Ruth Johnson in Haleyville on the day that a plaque in his honor was unveiled.

hood home had long ago been torn down. So had the house where Ruth had lived.

A hot wind blew through the shaded lawn, making the American flag snap smartly above them.

This day in Haleyville was a special one for Judge Johnson. Some of his old boyhood friends came by to shake his hand and spend a few moments recalling the distant past.

It was also a notable day because it would be Frank Johnson's last trip to the town.

In the final years of his life, he would spend hours in the back yard feeding and watching the birds. He had stopped hearing cases in 1995.

Then in 1999, the judge fell and broke a hip. He got pneumonia. On July 16, at age 80, Judge Johnson died. He was buried in Haleyville.

Over the years many have said that Judge Johnson was "the Abraham Lincoln of the 20th Century." Lincoln had freed the slaves, and Johnson, a hundred years later, had given the Alabama descendants of those slaves the full freedom of American citizenship. He was an Alabama judge, but the decisions he issued from the courtroom in Montgomery brought a wind of freedom across the land.

Frank M. Johnson, Jr.: Courageous Judge
Frank M. Johnson, Jr.

October 30, 1918 Frank Johnson is born in Delmar, Ala., near Haleyville.

January 16, 1938 Marries Ruth Jenkins.

September 1939 Ruth and Frank enroll at the University of Alabama.

August 1943 Enters the Army. He is sent to France as a lieutenant, and is twice wounded in combat. His wife, Ruth, joined the Navy a few months before he enlisted.

August 1946 Frank and Ruth return to Alabama, moving to Jasper where he joins the law firm of Curtis and Maddox.

May 1953 Chosen to be the U.S. Attorney for Northern Alabama.

November 7, 1955 Sworn in as the U.S. district judge in Montgomery; Alabama President Eisenhower had nominated him in October.

December 1, 1955 Rosa Parks is arrested on a bus for refusing to give her seat to a white man, starting the Montgomery Bus Boycott, the first event of the Civil Rights Movement.

May 11, 1956 Johnson, as part of a three-judge panel, hears the boycott case. He rules segregation violates the Constitution. Judge Rives agrees with him. The Supreme Court later upholds their opinion.

January 15. 1958 Orders state officials, including George Wallace, to turn over voting records to a federal agency.

February 17, 1961 Orders voting officials to begin registering blacks to be voters in Macon and Bullock counties.

May 29, 1961 Hears the Freedom Rider case, and threatens to send police officials, civil rights leaders, and Klan leaders to prison if there are any other skirmishes such as occurred at bus stations in Alabama.

1961 Declares the state poll tax—a tax that citizens had to pay to have the right to vote—is illegal.

Frank M. Johnson, Jr.: Courageous Judge

June 1963 Rules that Montgomery must desegregate its parks and the YMCA.

September 1963 Rules Macon County schools must desegregate.

March 11, 1965 In the Selma to Montgomery march case, Johnson rules the march can be held because the wrongs the marchers protested were "enormous."

December 3, 1965 Hears the KKK conspiracy case involving the death of Viola Liuzzo. Three KKK members are found guilty.

1971 Orders the state to upgrade mental health facilities.

1972 Orders the Alabama State Troopers to be desegregated until its force is 25 percent black.

1972 Orders the state to hire workers in a nondiscriminatory basis.

1972 Rules that women in the military have the same rights as men.

1974 Rules that the state must provide minimal standards for prisoners.

1977 President Carter nominates Johnson to head the FBI. But the judge's health problems force him to withdraw his name.

1979 Named to the U.S. 5th Circuit Court of Appeals.

1992 The federal building in Montgomery is renamed in Johnson's honor.

1995 Retires. President Clinton honors him with the Presidential Medal of Freedom.

July 16, 1999 Judge Johnson dies. He is buried in Haleyville, his hometown. His wife, Ruth, dies in 2008. She is buried beside him.

Frank M. Johnson, Jr.: Courageous Judge

About The Authors

Michelle Batcheler is a television broadcast major at the University of Alabama at Birmingham, with a minor in journalism. While a student, she also worked for *The Birmingham News*, WBRC-TV, and as a lifeguard for the YMCA.

Frank Sikora is a retired newspaper reporter, having worked in Alabama for 40 years. His work has appeared in *Time*, *Redbook* and *Parade* magazines. He has written five books.

This is their second book together. The first was a novel titled *The Visitor At Winter Chapel*.